A Challenge
to all Christians

By the same author

A Challenge
to all Christians

What it really means to be a disciple

Peter J. Southgate

First published 2015

Acknowledgements

All quotations, unless otherwise indicated, are taken from the
New King James Version®. Copyright © 1982 by Thomas Nelson.

Abbreviations

ESV English Standard Version
KJV King James Version
NIV New International Version
NKJV New King James Version
NLT New Living Translation

ISBN 978-1-874508-55-7

Published by the Dawn Book Supply
5 Station Road, Carlton, Nottingham NG4 3AT, England
www.dawnbooksupply.co.uk
Printed and bound in Great Britain

Contents

Author's preface

Brought up in a God-fearing, Christian family, my contact with the Bible gradually developed from the reading of children's Bible stories at an early age to a lifetime of regular daily contact with its pages. This has resulted in a love for, and appreciation of, its contents, outlining as they do the great plan that God has for the world and individuals through the saving work of the Lord Jesus Christ.

It is sad, therefore, to note that in many areas the Bible's clear teaching has been altered in ways that render the true Christian message confusing and in some cases unintelligible.

Now an octogenarian, and whilst my faculties still remain, it is my wish in love and friendship to ask my fellow Christians to seriously look at where they stand in relation to the message of Christianity as originally taught by the Lord Jesus. It is incumbent on all Christians to "earnestly contend for the faith which was once for all delivered to the saints" (Jude 3).

The issues raised in the following pages are not comprehensive, but address some major points on which I invite you to carefully and prayerfully reflect.

My thanks are due to several who have commented on my original drafts, to Ros Wall for her proofreading and to Emma Perfitt for the layout and cover design.

This little work is offered with the prayer that it will be to the honour of Him to whom all praise is due.

P.J.S.

Chapter 1
What is the basis of your Christian life?

So you're a Christian! Excellent! You are one of more than two billion people throughout the world who also claim the name.

By definition a Christian is a follower of Jesus Christ. Does that also apply to you? "Of course it does," you say. "I go to church. I try to live a good life, being kind and helpful as Jesus showed us."

Sounds good – and so it is.

But is that quite enough? Do you really know what Jesus taught and what he asks from those who claim to follow him? Or have you sheltered under the umbrella provided by official church teaching and not investigated things for yourself?

This book is a deliberate challenge to every Christian, of whatever race, colour or creed. How strong is your belief in Christ? How firm are your Christian foundations? What hope does Christianity hold out to you for this life – and the next? How sure can you be of what it offers?

A question of authority

I don't know if you have ever experienced this, but when I chat to people about what they believe and why they believe it, they so often start by saying: "Well, I think...". Often they have excellent and firmly based reasons for what they then go on to say, but sometimes these personal views of the different people I talk to are so divergent that one wonders whether all of them can be true.

So, is "what I think" enough when our eternal future is at stake? More important, where can we turn to for a really authoritative statement on Christian beliefs?

Probably most will look to their church. "I'll ask the vicar", or "I'll talk to the priest". Each of the major denominations has a clearly laid down set of beliefs and practices that have developed over many years. It could be thought that with these available the pastor or priest should easily settle the matter for any enquirer.

But one of the problems is that throughout Christianity these statements, or creeds as they are called, differ in several fundamental aspects. The Roman Church has one set of beliefs and rules, the Church of England has another that differs considerably and the Orthodox Catholic Church has yet other variations. Why the differences? As the Apostle Paul said: *"Is Christ divided?"*[1] Each of the differing sections of Christianity believes that its view is correct, otherwise they would all unite. And the other disturbing thing is that many claim divine guidance by the Holy Spirit. How can that be when they are so different? The Bible says: *"God is not the author of confusion"*,[2] so why the variations?

There clearly needs to be some firmer foundation, and we have it in what the nineteenth-century British Prime Minister Gladstone termed: "The impregnable rock of Holy Scripture".

But you will probably say: "All the organised churches accept the absolute authority of the Bible". Yes, they do, but often only in theory. They are content to deviate from the Bible's teaching when they perceive the need. Long-held traditions sometimes take precedence over Scripture.

The very basic feature of a real Christian must be that he or she follows Jesus in what he taught and the sort of life he lived. The word "disciple" means just that – "a follower". Christ's comment is very relevant – and soul-searching: *"Why do you call me*

---

1. 1 Corinthians 1.13   **2.** 1 Corinthians 14.33

'Lord, Lord,' and not do the things which I say?"[1] So in these pages let's put church teaching alongside the teaching of Jesus.

Jesus and the Old Testament

It's easy to forget that Christ's only Bible was what is now called the Old Testament, consisting of 39 separate "books", mainly concerned with God's dealings with the nation of Israel. Because much of it is ancient history many people regard it as irrelevant to modern Christianity, although admitting that it contains some moral guidance.

So what did Jesus – the one whose disciple you claim to be – have to say about his Bible, today called the Old Testament? He made some very important pronouncements about it:

- He calls it *"the word of God".*[2]

- It is absolutely reliable: *"The scripture cannot be broken"*;[3] *"All things must be fulfilled which were written in the Law of Moses and the Prophets and the Psalms".*[4]

- He used it as a basis of his teaching. Three times he refuted his tempter with *"It is written"*, before quoting from the book of Deuteronomy. He repeatedly rounded on his opponents with *"Have you not read..."* before going on to allude to an Old Testament incident.[5]

Christ's complete reliance on the Old Testament is shared by all the New Testament writers. Their teaching, without exception, is based firmly on the events and the instruction contained in the Old Testament. The Apostle Paul actually said that these "holy scriptures" of the Old Testament, all of which were given by "inspiration of God", could make the

---

1. Luke 6.46 **2.** Mark 7.13; Luke 4.4; John 10.35 **3.** John 10.35 **4.** Luke 24.44.
5. Matthew 12.3; 21.16; 22.31

reader "wise for salvation"[1] – something all Christians are striving for.

Do you know that the New Testament has 350 direct quotations from the Old Testament and over 600 allusions to events it records? Even more important, as we will show later, the New Testament firmly bases the true Christian hope on certain events described in the Old Testament.

Jesus, your leader and founder of your faith, accepted this vital importance of the Old Testament. Is this also your view? Do you share his opinion? Many who claim to follow Christ say that the Old Testament was a book for the Jews and is now irrelevant because the New Testament has superseded it. But do they know better than Jesus?

As a professed follower of Jesus, where do you stand on this?

What about the New Testament?

"We're on much firmer ground here", you might say: "This is the real textbook for Christianity." But do you accept it implicitly and in its entirety? Although the New Testament was not actually written until after Jesus had gone to heaven, his influence on all its contents and his endorsement of its teaching is immense.

Here are just some of the comments by Jesus and his Apostles:

Just before he ascended to heaven Jesus promised his disciples that the Holy Spirit would *"guide you into all truth"*.[2] He further said that the Holy Spirit would *"teach you all things, and bring to your remembrance all things that I said to you"*.[3] Thus, all the pronouncements by the writers of the New Testament were guided by the Holy Spirit, so all that they said and wrote must therefore be regarded as accurate and authoritative.

---

1. 1 Timothy 3.15–16 **2.** John 16.13 **3.** John 14.26

Because of this Holy Spirit guidance the writers of the New Testament claimed divine authority for what they taught. The Apostle Paul told the Galatian church that, *"the gospel which was preached by me is not according to man. For I neither received it from man, nor was I taught it, but it came through the revelation of Jesus Christ."*[1] So Jesus personally told Paul what he wanted him to preach. Thus, Paul could insist that the things he wrote were not pushing his own ideas (as some today disparagingly suggest), but were in fact the direct teaching of Jesus. As he said: *"The things which I write to you are the commandments of the Lord."*[2]

In his inspired letter, the foremost of Christ's disciples, Peter, puts Paul's writings on a par with the then existing Scriptures, the Old Testament.[3]

An integrated book

Thus, the original Christians firmly believed that all of what we now call the Bible, consisting of Old and New Testaments, was a God-sent and therefore completely accurate and reliable basis for Christian life and beliefs.

As a Christian in the twenty-first century, can you honestly say that this is also your firmly held view of the Bible? Or do you pick and choose which parts of the Bible you accept and respond to?

If you do, what is the basis for your selection? Do you go along with those who say that we have now moved on, and that we should adapt our beliefs to the changing times?

These are important questions, because in the very last chapter of the Bible Jesus himself gives a stern warning to

---

1. Galatians 1.11–12 **2.** 1 Corinthians 14.37 **3.** 2 Peter 3.15–16

any who would add to or water down its message: *"For I testify to everyone who hears the words of the prophecy of this book: if anyone adds to these things, God will add to him the plagues that are written in this book; and if anyone takes away from the words of the book of this prophecy, God shall take away his part from the Book of Life, from the holy city, and from the things which are written in this book."*[1]

With this foundation we can now look at some specific aspects of Bible teaching in relation to current Christian belief.

---

1. Revelation 22.18–19

Chapter 2
Have you an immortal soul?

One of the most popular broadcasts at Christmas is the Festival of Nine Lessons and Carols from King's College Chapel at Cambridge, UK. The Dean's prayer at the commencement includes the following: "Lastly let us remember before God all those who rejoice with us, but upon another shore and in a greater light." This highlights the universal belief that at death an immaterial essence residing in people, usually termed the "soul", leaves the body and continues a conscious existence elsewhere. This belief has been so ingrained into Christian thought over nearly 2000 years that it is regarded as an absolutely basic doctrine.

But what would you say if I told you that it is not taught in the Bible? True, the word "soul" appears often, but never, repeat never, the words "immortal soul".

Don't be misled by this word "soul". In the original language in which the Bible was written it simply means something that is alive. It is applied to animals as well as humans. We often use the word in everyday speech to describe the actual person rather than some immaterial essence. When terrified passengers on a sinking ship sent out the distress call SOS, "save our souls", they were calling for a lifeboat, not the saving offices of a clergyman.

Sometimes in the Bible the word "soul" is also used to denote some activities of living things, such as thoughts or feelings – but all these activities cease when the living creature dies. The Bible is adamant that existence and thought ceases at death. Think on these passages:

- *"For the living know that they will die; but the dead know nothing"*; *"There is no work or device or knowledge or wisdom in the grave where you are going".*[1]

- In the Psalms, David was inspired by God to write: *"For in death there is no remembrance of you* [God]; *in the grave who will give you thanks?"*[2] He also wrote that when a man dies, *"he returns to his earth; in that very day his plans perish".*[3] He also refers to the grave as *"the land of forget-fulness".*[4] No idea of a continued existence here.

- In both Old and New Testaments, death is consistently referred to as "a sleep". On the death of loved ones the Bible never consoles believers with the assurance that the departed are now living a better life. Rather, they are regarded as simply asleep in the grave. The true Christian hope is in resurrection from the dead. This is the way in which Christ and Paul comforted the bereaved of their day. Thus, Martha said of her dead brother Lazarus: *"I know that he will rise again in the resurrection at the last day."*[5]

- Have you ever thought it incongruous that if the departed Lazarus was enjoying a fuller and happier life in heaven then why were his sisters so sad, and why did Jesus bring him back to this vale of tears?

- And what of Paul's comfort to the Christians in Thessalonica? If they had been taught that their departed loved ones had been transported to a fuller life and were praising God in heaven, why would they need these words of comfort and reassurance to alleviate their sorrow? *"But I do not want you to be ignorant, brethren, concerning those who have fallen asleep, lest you sorrow as others who have no hope... For the Lord Himself will descend from heaven with a shout, with the voice of an archangel, and with the*

---

1. Ecclesiastes 9.5,10 **2.** Psalm 6.5 **3.** Psalm 146.4 **4.** Psalm 88.12 **5.** John 11.24

trumpet of God. And the dead in Christ will rise first."[1]

Note that these references contain the key to the Bible's teaching about life after death. Only after the resurrection, will eternal life be granted to those who at Christ's judgement seat are deemed faithful.

The fact that Christians will appear at some sort of tribunal to be either rewarded or punished is consistent Bible teaching. Here is just a selection:

- *"And many of those who sleep in the dust of the earth shall awake. Some to everlasting life, some to shame and everlasting contempt".*[2]

- *"For we must all appear before the judgment seat of Christ, that each one may receive the things done in the body, according to what he has done, whether good or bad".*[3]

This makes sense of an otherwise illogical situation. If a Christian's reward is immediate on his death, why is he later resurrected, then judged to see if he or she ought to have received that reward?

If you have any doubts about people possessing immortal souls I would like to give you the words of William Tyndale. He was the sixteenth-century translator of the Bible into English, so he ought to have known just what it contained. He said, when debating with a Roman priest in 1535: "Ye, in putting departed souls in heaven, hell, and purgatory, destroy the arguments wherewith Christ and Paul prove the resurrection... If the dead are already in a blissful paradise, why must there yet be a resurrection?"

---

1. 1 Thessalonians 4.13, 16 **2.** Daniel 12.2 **3.** 2 Corinthians 5.10

John Wesley, the famous founder of the Methodist Church, had the same view: "It is indeed generally supposed that the souls of good men as soon as dislodged from the body, go directly to heaven, but this opinion has not the least foundation in the oracles of God... We are in good company when we stand firmly upon the Bible truth that man is a mortal creature, who sleeps in death, and whose only hope for conscious existence after death is in resurrection to immortality when Jesus comes again."

Where did the idea of an immortal soul originate?

If it is not found in the Bible from where did the idea of an immortal soul come? The concept of the soul's supposed immortality was taught in ancient Egypt and Babylon. It was developed further by Greek philosophers in the fifth and fourth centuries BC, especially by Plato. In the years between the Old and New Testaments, the Jews, despite the teaching of their sacred book the Bible, readily accepted it. As one authority says: "The belief in the immortality of the soul came to the Jews from contact with Greek thought and chiefly through the philosophy of Plato, its principal exponent."[1] Christ's parable of the rich man and Lazarus was directed against the Jewish leaders of his day who had accepted this non-scriptural belief.[2]

Early Christianity was also influenced and corrupted by the same Greek philosophies and by AD 200 the doctrine of the immortality of the soul became adopted by Christian believers. Origen (185–253), regarded as one of the early church fathers, strongly advocated the doctrine, having himself been influenced by these Greek thinkers.[3] Later, Augustine (354–430) taught that death meant the destruction of the body, but the conscious soul would continue to live in either a blissful

---

1. *Jewish Encyclopedia*, 1941, Vol. 6, "Immortality of the Soul", pp. 564, 566
2. Luke 16.19–31 3. See, for example, *The Evangelical Dictionary of Theology,* 1992, "Soul", p.1037

state with God or an agonising state of separation from God.

This belief soon became widespread, and in 1513, at the fifth Lateran Council, Pope Leo X pronounced the doctrine of the immortality of the soul to be a fundamental Christian doctrine. He then issued a Papal Bull that condemned all who would deny the individual immortality of the human soul or suggest doubts on these matters. Incidentally, it was this Bull that provoked the response by William Tyndale quoted earlier.

And this error is still taught. In the current Church of England "Order of service for the burial of the dead" a prayer is recommended which commences: "Almighty God, with whom do live the spirits of them that depart hence in the Lord, and with whom the souls of the faithful, after they are delivered from the burden of the flesh, are in joy and felicity."

What is your reaction to all this? Do you, as a Christian, pin your hope for the future on something that was not taught by your leader and is not found in God's inspired Word? Do you realise that in believing in an immortal soul you are not following Christ, but merely the human reasoning of ancient pagan nations and some old Greek philosophers?

If you dispute the foregoing conclusions you can check their validity by accessing "immortal soul" in any Internet search engine.

In fact, the belief that humans have an immortal soul is the cardinal error of almost all the world's religions, not only Christianity. As such, it even has political ramifications, for do not many terrorists fervently believe that their murderous actions gain for them immediate access to heaven? But in this book we are addressing Christians, and saying that by their acceptance of this fundamental error many other wrong doctrines have been built, such as hell torments and heaven-going, which we will consider next.

Accepting overall Bible teaching

At this point it is worth making the general comment that if one comes to the Bible with preconceived ideas it is sometimes possible to find a few verses that appear to support them. But that is entirely different from coming to the Bible with an open mind to learn what it really teaches. An example is the one mentioned earlier – Christ's parable of the rich man and Lazarus. Superficially, this suggests that both these characters had a continued existence after death. But in fact Jesus was not defining the state of the dead but using the wrong beliefs of the Jewish leaders to make a telling point concerning his resurrection. Ambiguous passages or those with abstract meanings must never be used to disagree with straightforward Bible statements. I will often refer to this point in later pages.

Chapter 3
Rewards: heaven or hell?

In a medieval church near where I live there is a famous painting, dating from the twelfth century, that covers the wall at one end of the building (see below). It depicts in graphic detail the respective fates of the wicked and the righteous. The upper half represents heaven, into which the faithful are ushered by the angels. The lower half shows hell, where demons roast the wicked over fires or prod them as they stew in vats of boiling oil.

Obviously, if people do not have an immortal soul that lives on at death and which therefore has to be sent somewhere, then belief in scenes such as this is a non-starter. I have already demonstrated that this is the case, but you may still have reservations because of ingrained beliefs and the frequent mention of hell in the Bible, together with some occasional allusions that might support heaven-going.

Many today would suggest that pictures such as the above were the product of a more superstitious and less tolerant age, when ignorant worshippers were frightened into obedience.

But the threat of dire punishment for the unfaithful in a burning hell was still being routinely taught until comparatively recent times. Charles Spurgeon (1834–92), a very prominent London preacher, made it a dominant feature of his sermons:

> We do not care about metaphorical fires. But they are real, sir – yes, as real as yourself. There is a real fire in hell, as truly as you have now a real body – a fire exactly like that which we have on earth in everything except this – that it will not consume, though it will torture you. You have seen the asbestos lying in the fire red hot, but when you take it out it is unconsumed. So your body will be prepared by God in such a way that it will burn for ever without being consumed; it will lie, not as you consider, in metaphorical fire, but in actual flame.

Of recent years, such belief in hell fire and eternal torment of the wicked has been very much soft-pedalled. Even the Roman Catholic Church's very long-standing belief in hell torments has been challenged by the current Pontiff, Francis. "The church no longer believes in a literal hell where people suffer", he said in a speech in 2013. (What then of the "papal infallibility" in doctrinal matters of previous centuries?)

But, you might say: "Are there not many references to hell throughout the Bible?" Yes, indeed! But the great majority of these use the word "hell" to describe nothing more than "the grave". The English word originally denoted simply a "covering up". It is derived from Old English *hel*, or *helle* (about 725), which comes from Proto-Germanic *halja*, meaning "one who covers up or hides something", which is what one does when burying a body. It is interesting that the Hebrew word *sheol* is translated in the KJV as "grave" exactly the same number of times as it is "hell", suggesting an equivalent meaning. So the occurrence of the word "hell" in the Bible does not normally denote a place of fiery torment, simply a hidden place, the grave.

The belief in hell-fire torments arose from a misunderstanding of an allusion of Christ. He said that the wicked *"go to hell, into the fire that shall never be quenched – where their worm does not die, and the fire is not quenched"*.[1]

Jesus is here using a special word whose meaning his hearers would have easily understood, although many translations of the Bible do not indicate the distinction. This word is *gehenna* and refers to a specific place on the outskirts of Jerusalem. "Gehenna", or "gehinnom" is composed of two Hebrew words, *ge* meaning "valley" and *hinnom*, the name of a person connected with that place. This "valley of the son of Hinnom" was immediately south of the walls of Jerusalem and is frequently mentioned in the Old Testament.[2] In the days of the kings in Jerusalem this valley was used for horrific child sacrifices, when infants were burnt alive in a "Tophet" sacrifice to the false gods.[3]

Jewish tradition reveals that in Christ's day a burning rubbish heap in the Valley of Hinnom gave rise to the idea of a fiery place of judgement. They maintained that in this valley fires were kept burning perpetually (hence the "not quenched" reference of Jesus) to consume the refuse of Jerusalem, including the corpses of criminals. The edges of this decaying rubbish attracted flies, whose maggots were continually present (hence "where their worm does not die"). The point of this allusion is that nothing put into this conflagration would survive, and so Jesus used it as a symbol of the complete destruction of the unfaithful.

---

1. Mark 9.43–44 **2.** Jeremiah 19.2 *et al.* **3.** Jeremiah 7.31 *et al.*

A similar symbol, the "lake of fire", is used in the Book of Revelation to describe the annihilation of the wicked for eternity.[1]

Thus, the "gehenna" hell of the New Testament is a symbol for the eternal complete destruction of the unfaithful, not a literal place of everlasting torment.

Going to heaven at death

Most of us have experienced intense sorrow at the loss of a loved one. The sorrow is even greater if it is a young person or a child. How often the mourners are consoled by the assurance that their dear ones are in a far better place.

In a stroll around my local cemetery I noted the following sentiments on the gravestones:

- "If tears could build a stairway we'd walk right up to heaven and bring you home again"

- "Death is only a shadow across the path to heaven"

- "Our precious angel shining down on us from heaven"; "As you play among the angels"

- "As the bird free of its cage seeks the heights so the Christian soul in death flies home to God"

- "Promoted to glory"

Such sentiments are widely believed in most Christian communities and are supported by official church statements, as in the *English Prayer Book*.

It is impossible not to feel sincere sympathy with those whose loved ones have died. At such times all possible consolation

---

1. Revelation 21.8; 20.10

needs to be offered to the bereaved. But, we ask, if heaven is the immediate reward at death, where is the direct statement of this fact in Scripture? Surely it would be the one thing that Christ and his Apostles would have preached and used to console mourners in their times of sadness.

The Apostle Paul faced this very situation in his day and spelt out very clearly the true Christian hope: *"I do not want you to be ignorant, brethren, concerning those who have fallen asleep, lest you sorrow as others who have no hope."* How, then, did he dispel their ignorance? Was it by telling them that their loved ones were in heaven? Not a bit of it! The hope he offered was that they would come to life again at the return of Jesus: *"For the Lord Himself will descend from heaven with a shout, with the voice of an archangel, and with the trumpet of God. And the dead in Christ will rise first… Therefore comfort one another with these words."*[1]

The consistent Bible teaching, as we have already seen[2] is that we possess no immortal soul; death is the end of all consciousness and the real Christian hope lies in resurrection.

One of the great Old Testament characters is David, termed by Scripture: *"A man after his* [God's] *own heart".*[3] He was the *"sweet psalmist of Israel"* who rightly claimed that: *"the Spirit of the Lord spoke by me".*[4] So what divine message of hope did David have for his readers? In a psalm contrasting the alternative fates of the righteous and the wicked he never mentions heaven, but repeatedly says that the reward for faithfulness will be on earth – that is, after a resurrection:

•   *"For evildoers shall be cut off; but those who wait on the LORD, they shall inherit the earth"*

---

1.   1 Thessalonians 4.13, 16, 18 **2.** Chapter 2 **3.** 1 Samuel 13.14; Acts 13.22
4. 2 Samuel 23.1–2

- *"But the meek shall inherit the earth"*

- *"For those blessed by Him shall inherit the earth"*[1]

In the New Testament this future reward on earth rather than in heaven is repeated by none other than Jesus himself, who in his famous Sermon on the Mount actually quotes these same words of David: *"Blessed are the meek, for they shall inherit the earth."* [2]

And to confirm that this is the correct understanding we have the words of the Apostle Peter, who specifically states that after he was *"dead and buried… David did not ascend into the heavens"*.[3] If the man after God's own heart did not go to heaven, how can we claim that lesser mortals do?

So we ask: how does this square with the opening prayer at the Christmas carol service which speaks of the redeemed being in heaven "on another shore and in a greater light"?

As one who professes to follow Christ you must face up to this. You cannot have both views. If the Bible is right and the dead do not immediately wing their way to heaven, then the centuries-old belief as epitomised in that old church painting is a pious fable.

But what about…

But, you might say: "Did not Christ speak of our 'reward in heaven' and on the cross promised the thief immediate translation to paradise? And does not Paul refer also to our 'reward in heaven' and mentions his desire to 'depart and be with Christ'?" I would here like to refer back to my earlier comment, that if one approaches the Bible with pre-formed views it is sometimes possible to find support for them – but at

---

1. Psalm 37.9, 11, 22 **2.** Matthew 5.5 **3.** Acts 2.29, 34

the expense of the whole direction of the rest of Bible teaching.

"Great is your reward in heaven"

So let's look at some of these references. First, three with similar wording:

- Jesus said: *"Rejoice and be exceedingly glad, for great is your reward in heaven"*[1]

- *"Go, sell what you have and give to the poor, and you will have treasure in heaven"*[2]

- Paul wrote: *"The hope which is laid up for you in heaven"*[3]

Undoubtedly, the reward at present is located in heaven, but there are two possible ways by which that reward might be reached – either by us going up to heaven, as so many Christians believe and teach, or by the reward coming down from heaven to us. The second possibility is what the Bible teaches. Jesus clearly stated that the reward would be given at his return to the earth: *"For the Son of Man will come in the glory of his Father with his angels, and then he will reward each according to his works."*[4]

The thief in paradise

But, you may say, "What about the dying thief on the cross? Jesus said to him: *'I say to you, today you will be with me in paradise.'*[5] Doesn't that mean that the thief gained his reward that very day?"

Let's think carefully about this passage again, not jumping to conclusions. Where did Jesus and the thief **actually go** on the very day of their crucifixion? Was it to paradise (whatever that

---

1. Matthew 5.12 2. Matthew 19.21 3. Colossians 1.5
4. Matthew 16.27. See also Colossians 3.4; Revelation 22.12 5. Luke 23.43

may mean)? No, it is quite clear that both went to the grave (the hell of the Bible) and Jesus stayed there for three days. Not much of an instant reward for Jesus or the thief.

Also notice that the thief said nothing about going to heaven. His request related to the future: *"Lord, remember me when you come into your kingdom."*[1] He was not asking for immediate reward but for participation in some future event. He had probably heard Christ preaching about his future kingdom when paradise would be restored on earth and he was asking for a place in it. Jesus solemnly promised that his request would then be granted.

A fourth–century Greek copy of the Bible

"But", you may continue, "why did Jesus say, 'today', suggesting that the thief would receive his reward the same day that he died?" The answer is quite simple. Many readers of the Bible do not know that in the Greek manuscripts there is no punctuation, capital letters or even spaces between words. Christ's words thus appear as: "isaytoyoutodayyouwillbewithmeinparadise" This rarely is a problem for translators, but sometimes can lead to differences in punctuation. Christ's reply to the thief is a case in point. It can legitimately be translated with the comma in a different place. Instead of, *"I say to you, today you will..."* it could equally be: *"I say to you today, you will..."*. This is more in keeping with the thief's request. He wanted to be assured that at some future time (*"when you come into your kingdom"*)

---

1. Luke 23.42

he would be remembered. But Jesus tells him that he need not wait until then for such an assurance: he would give it to him there and then. Jesus comforted him that instant with the promise that he would definitely be rewarded when Christ's future Kingdom comes.

"Depart and be with Christ"

Here are words from Paul's pen that superficially seem to suggest an immediate transition at death. Whilst a prisoner in chains he wrote to the Colossians that although he would quite happily die for his faith, his continued presence would be of more benefit to them: *"For to me, to live is Christ, and to die is gain… For I am hard-pressed between the two, having a desire to depart and be with Christ, which is far better. Nevertheless to remain in the flesh is more needful for you."*[1]

As with other similar references, the crucial point relates to the timing. Paul is not saying that after his death he will immediately be with Christ. We must allow Paul to be consistent in his writings. Later on in the very same epistle he unambiguously spells out that his hope for the future was not immediately at his death but at the return of Jesus to the earth to give him immortality: *"For our citizenship*[2] *is in heaven, from which we also eagerly wait for the Savior, the Lord Jesus Christ, who will transform our lowly body that it may be conformed to his glorious body, according to the working by which he is able even to subdue all things to himself."*[3] Thus, Paul's hope was centred on the return of Jesus. But he also knew that as death resulted in complete unconsciousness, the transition to the presence of Christ in effect would appear to be immediately at his death. At his next conscious moment he would be "with Christ".

---

1. Philippians 1.21–24   **2.** A Greek term for "the constitution of a commonwealth, form of government and the laws by which it is administered", *Vine's Greek Lexicon*
3. Philippians 3.20–21

Thus, we cannot use this isolated reference by Paul (and there is a similar one in his letter to the Corinthians[1]) to go against his own clear teaching and indeed the whole of scriptural revelation on the topic.

"In my Father's house..."

Another frequently quoted passage to support heaven-going at death is Christ's reference in John 14: *"In My Father's house are many mansions; if it were not so, I would have told you. I go to prepare a place for you."*[2] Here, it is assumed that "My Father's house" refers to heaven.

But Jesus never used this term to describe heaven. On the only previous occasion when he used "My Father's house" it referred to the temple in Jerusalem.[3] So, here again, to suggest that this teaches heaven-going at death is something based on a prior assumption. Bible teaching is that God's house is not heaven but is a spiritual building made up of the faithful believers. The Apostle Peter says: *"You also, as living stones, are being built up a spiritual house, a holy priesthood, to offer up spiritual sacrifices acceptable to God through Jesus Christ."*[4] Jesus promises: *"He who overcomes, I will make him a pillar in the temple of my God."*[5] The Apostle Paul makes a similar reference: *"Now, therefore, you are... built on the foundation of the apostles and prophets, Jesus Christ himself being the chief cornerstone, in whom the whole building, being fitted together, grows into a holy temple in the Lord, in whom you also are being built together for a dwelling place of God in the spirit."*[6]

Christ is not promising that his going to heaven is to prepare a place into which the believers can follow. Rather, Jesus is saying that whilst in heaven he is preparing this world

---

1. 2 Corinthians 5.6   2. John 14.2   3. Luke 2.49, NIV   4. 1 Peter 2.5
5. Revelation 3.12   6. Ephesians 2.19–22

and his followers for inclusion in the community in which God will dwell. Note that Jesus then goes on to say that this union with him will take place at his second coming: *"And if I go and prepare a place for you **I will come again and receive you to myself**; that where I am, there you may be also."*[1] We must not base a belief on the first phrase and ignore the second.

I am truly sorry if looking at this topic has dashed some fervently held hopes. But as a twentieth–century psychologist once said in a different context: "Illusions commend themselves to us because they save us pain and allow us to enjoy pleasure instead. We must therefore accept it without complaint when they sometimes collide with a bit of reality against which they are dashed to pieces."[2]

---

1. John 14.3 **2.** Sigmund Freud

Chapter 4
What is the Kingdom of God?

The Kingdom of God was the main thrust of the preaching of Christ and his Apostles. From the many references in the New Testament you can build up a picture of some of its features.

- It was "good news" – for that is what the word "gospel" means: *"And Jesus went about all Galilee, teaching in their synagogues, preaching the gospel of the kingdom."*[1]

- In Christ's day the Kingdom of God was still in the future: *"He spoke another parable, because He was near Jerusalem and because they thought the kingdom of God would appear immediately."*[2]

- It will arrive at the return of Jesus to the earth: *"The Lord Jesus Christ, who will judge the living and the dead at His appearing and His kingdom."*[3]

- Just before the Kingdom comes there will be indications that it is near: *"So you also, when you see these things happening, know that the kingdom of God is near."*[4]

- When it arrives some will enter, others will be excluded: *"There will be weeping and gnashing of teeth, when you see Abraham and Isaac and Jacob and all the prophets in the kingdom of God, and yourselves thrust out."*[5] *"Now the works of the flesh are evident… those who practice such things will not inherit the kingdom of God."*[6]

- Those who do enter must first be changed in some way: *"Now this I say, brethren, that flesh and blood cannot inherit the kingdom of God"*;[7] *"I say to you, unless one is born of*

---

1. Matthew 4.23   **2.** Luke 19.11   **3.** 2 Timothy 4.1   **4.** Luke 21.31   **5.** Luke 13.28
6. Galatians 5.19–21   **7.** 1 Corinthians 15.50

water and the spirit, he cannot enter the kingdom of God." [1]

- Jesus advised his followers to seek it as a matter of priority: *"Seek first the kingdom of God and His righteousness."* [2]

As we say, from these references you can get a fair idea of some of the basic things about the Kingdom of God. It is **yet future** – for Christ has not yet returned; entrance to it will be **selective**; and those judged worthy to be accepted into it will be **transformed** in some way before they can enter it.

Now I suggest that if you asked an average cross section of churchgoers what was the kingdom that their leader devoted his mission to talking about, you would get few responses that would tally with these basic Bible concepts.

What do you think? When you recite the Lord's prayer and say "Thy kingdom come" what are you asking for?

Do you say that the Kingdom of God is the Christian church? Or do you believe that it exists where Jesus rules in the believer's heart? Do you say that it is heaven, where God reigns and where the faithful go to be with Him? Or do you say that the Kingdom of God refers to a transformed earth that will result from Christ's second coming?

Please do a little experiment. Before you continue reading go back to the bullet pointed references above and replace the words "kingdom" or "kingdom of God" with what you have been taught to believe. For example, would changing "kingdom of God" to "a reign of grace in the heart" or "the church" make sense in **all** the references?

Please do that – it should make you think.

*****

---

1. John 3.5   2. Matthew 6.33

What did you find? I suggest that in all fairness you would have to say that the only concept that fits **all** the references is that the Kingdom of God is a yet future event occurring when Christ returns.

And this is just what the Bible teaches. The Old Testament predicts that sometime in the future, human kingdoms on earth will be replaced by a worldwide Kingdom of God. The prophet Daniel, after describing a succession of human kingdoms, predicts a time when all will be removed and replaced by a divine kingdom on the earth: *"The God of heaven will set up a kingdom which shall never be destroyed; and the kingdom shall not be left to other people; it shall break in pieces and consume all these* [i.e. human] *kingdoms, and it shall stand forever."*[1] And the final book of the Bible also tells of a future time when: *"The kingdoms of this world have become the kingdoms of our Lord and of His Christ, and He shall reign forever and ever."*[2]

This is all in keeping with the angel's assertion to the virgin Mary that her promised son would: *"reign over the house of Jacob* [i.e. Israel] *forever, and of his kingdom there will be no end"*.[3]

Jesus himself says that his kingdom will be established at his return to earth: *"When the Son of Man comes in his glory, and all the holy angels with Him,* **then** *he will sit on the throne of His glory."* He will then invite the faithful to enter that kingdom: *"Come, you blessed of my Father, inherit the kingdom prepared for you from the foundation of the world."*[4]

There is no doubt that these Bible passages tell of a future

---

1. Daniel 2.44   2. Revelation 11.15   3. Luke 1.33   4. Matthew 25.31, 34

literal kingdom on earth, with Jesus as its king and into which the faithful will be invited to enter.

But what about…?

As we have intimated, many Christians have alternative understandings about the Kingdom of God – and even if they have some hazy views that it may also include some yet future events, such events are very far off and so remote from modern times as to have no personal impact.

A state of grace

One piously held view is that the Kingdom of God refers to the state of grace existing in the heart of a believer when Christ reigns there. For example, the *Catholic Encyclopaedia* says: "The 'kingdom' means Christ's reign of grace in men's hearts", and this view is widespread among all Christian churches.

But do you know that this is based on just one comment by Jesus – and that is taken out of context? This should make us prick up our ears, for doctrine based on one verse and not confirmed elsewhere in Scripture (let alone being actually contradicted by other Scripture) should make us pause. But the almost inevitable response when the view is questioned is: "Did not Jesus say *'The kingdom of God is within you'*?"

Yes, so it is recorded. But rather than divorce Christ's words from their context, let's read the whole of the conversation as recorded by Luke: *"Now when he was asked by the Pharisees when the kingdom of God would come, he answered them and said, 'The kingdom of God does not come with observation; nor will they say, "See here!" or "See there!" For indeed, the kingdom of God is within you.'"*[1]

The first important thing to note is that Jesus was talking to his inveterate opponents, those hypocritical Pharisees that we read so much about in the gospels. It was to these that Jesus said: *"The kingdom of God is within you."* Yes, the evil Pharisees. So we ask: "Did Jesus reign in **their** hearts? Was the Kingdom of God in **them**?" Surely not! Here is how Jesus describes the contents of the Pharisees' hearts: *"Woe to you, scribes and Pharisees, hypocrites! For you are like whitewashed tombs, which indeed appear beautiful outwardly, but inside are full of dead men's bones and all uncleanness. Even so you also outwardly appear righteous to men, but inside you are full of hypocrisy and lawlessness."*[2] Is it really being suggested that these evil traits inside the Pharisees were characteristic of the Kingdom of God?

What did Jesus mean, then? The Pharisees had asked when the Kingdom of God would come, and Jesus' reply was that in one sense it had already arrived. Most modern translations correctly render Jesus' words as, *"The Kingdom of God is already among you"* (NLT) or, *"is in your midst"* (NIV, ESV, RSV). An intriguing reply admittedly, but Jesus rarely spoke plainly to the evil Pharisees. The Kingdom was in their midst in the sense that Jesus was there preaching about it and asking the people to accept this good news. As the opening chapter of Mark records, Jesus said: *"The kingdom of God is at hand. Repent, and believe in the gospel."*[3]

Another way of looking at Jesus' words has been suggested by Greek scholars. Manuscripts discovered from New Testament

---

1. Luke 17 20–21 **1.** Matthew 23.27–28 **2.** Mark 1.15

times throw light on the colloquial use of the word "within". It was an idiom[1] for "within reach". In an Egyptian papyrus dating from New Testament times a doctor writes that his cloak be sent up from the country so that he may have it "within him", obviously meaning "within my reach". He didn't intend to eat it.

So the fundamental meaning of "within you" is "having something within your reach", something that you have the power to grasp, rather than suggesting something actually inside a person. Jesus was telling the Pharisees that the Kingdom of God was accessible, within their grasp.

With this understanding, Christ's words tally with all the other Bible references to the kingdom of God.

The church is the Kingdom of God

Some Christians believe that the Kingdom of God is the church, the present community of believers. This was first propounded by the fourth–century Christian "father", Augustine. In his book *The City of God* he wrote: "Therefore even now the Church is the kingdom of Christ", and this view became widely accepted. The *Westminster Confession of Faith* states that: "The visible church... is the kingdom of the Lord Jesus Christ, the house and family of God, out of which there is no ordinary possibility of salvation."[2]

If asked for scriptural confirmation, these words of Paul are usually quoted: *"For he has rescued us from the dominion of darkness and brought us into the kingdom of the Son he loves."*[3]

---

1. An idiom is a word or phrase used to denote something different from its literal meaning. **2.** 25.2 **3.** Colossians 1.13 (NIV)

But bearing in mind the many references by Paul (and in the rest of the Bible) referring to the Kingdom as a future event, can we really use this to prove beyond doubt that the Kingdom exists now?

Again, the background is essential for the right understanding. Paul is here using contrasts that are regular features of his writings. Elsewhere he indicates that believers had changed masters;[1] they were "in Adam" but now "in Christ";[2] they were once "far off" but are now "brought near".[3] And in the same vein in this instance he makes the contrast between the "dominion of darkness" and "the kingdom of the Son". In other words, what Paul is saying is that the Christians had left their previous life and had been brought within the orbit of the things Jesus preached, things that were centred around a belief in the coming Kingdom.

That the first Christians, including Paul, regarded the Kingdom as a future development rather than an existing one is plain from the very many other references he made to it,[4] let alone the teaching of Jesus himself.

"My kingdom is not of this world"

"Ah yes", another may say, "But what about Christ's statement to Pilate: *'My kingdom is not of this world'.*[5] Surely that means that the kingdom is either in heaven or is a purely spiritual one?" But was Jesus by this contradicting the many clear references to his Kingdom we have considered earlier, or did he mean something else?

As always, the context helps us decide. Here is the full account of this exchange between Christ and his judge. Pilate said: *"Am I a Jew? Your own nation and the chief priests have delivered*

---

1. Romans 6.17, 18 **2.** 1 Corinthians 15.22 **3.** Ephesians 2.12, 13
4. 2 Peter 1.11; 2 Timothy 4.1; James 2.5; Galatians 5.21 **5.** John 18.36

you to me. What have you done?' Jesus answered, 'My kingdom is not of this world. If my kingdom were of this world, my servants would fight, so that I should not be delivered to the Jews; but now my kingdom is not from here.'"[1]

It all depends on what Jesus meant by "this world".

The situation was this. As Pilate said, the Jewish rulers and religious authorities had brought Jesus to trial on the pretext that he was a threat to Roman rule because he claimed to be king of the Jews. Hence Pilate's question: "Are you the king of the Jews?" Jesus did not deny this but said his kingship would be under a different administration.

It was the Jewish "world" of his day, with all its hypocrisy and formalism, that Jesus was repudiating. The original word for "world" in this verse is *kosmos* – a Greek word that means: "an apt and harmonious arrangement or constitution, order, government".[2] The word is used for the **arrangement** of things on the earth rather than referring to the actual planet, for which in Greek there is a different word. So Jesus was telling Pilate that his kingship was not of this arrangement of things. His mission was not an attempt to immediately revive the old Jewish monarchy or perpetuate the Jewish system of worship, but would be a future *kosmos* or arrangement, as he had consistently preached during his mission. And indeed Christ's coming Kingdom will be truly "out of this world" in the sense that we often use the phrase.

Thus, a closer look at some of the popular ideas concerning the Kingdom of God shows that a true understanding of the Bible's message does not support many of them, however sincerely they may be held.

---

1. John 18.35–36 **2.** *Strong's Concordance*

We now proceed to look at another aspect of first-century preaching that is largely ignored by Christians today, one that is closely related to the teaching about the Kingdom of God.

Chapter 5
The "covenants of promise"

If you, as a church-going Christian, were asked: "What are the covenants of promise?" how would you reply? Would you rack your brains, searching for an answer?

Yet they are something essential for your salvation: without them you have no hope. Paul wrote to his Gentile converts that before they were converted they were: *"without Christ, being aliens from the commonwealth of Israel and strangers from the covenants of promise, having no hope and without God in the world".*[1]

How many sermons have you heard explaining God's promise to some Old Testament characters in relation to the work of Christ? Not many, I suspect. Yet for the earliest Christians these promises were fundamental to their beliefs. Without them it was a case of "having no hope and without God in the world". Do you, as a twenty-first century Christian, know what these promises were?

To a Jew, and indeed to a first-century Christian, the "covenants of promise" meant only one thing. They were the promises that God made to Abraham and David. When Paul was on trial in Jerusalem, accused of being a Christian, he said to his Jewish opponents: *"And now I stand and am judged for the hope of the promise made by God to our fathers."*[2] And these promises to the Jewish fathers were not a side issue for Paul. It was the very basis of his preaching. Addressing his audience at Antioch he said of the famous King David: *"From this man's seed, **according to the promise**, God raised up for Israel a Saviour – Jesus."*[3] He ended his discourse by saying that this promise

---

1. Ephesians 2.12   2. Acts 26.6   3. Acts 13.23

concerning Jesus made to the Jewish fathers was good news for his listeners: *"And we declare to you glad tidings – that **promise** which was made to the fathers."* [1]

As Christians, we should surely want to know details of this promise that God made to King David concerning Jesus. It involved the coming of his very special descendant: *"When your days are fulfilled and you rest with your fathers, I will set up your seed after you, who will come from your body, and I will establish his kingdom. He shall build a house for my name, and I will establish the throne of his kingdom forever. I will be his Father, and he shall be my son... And your house and your kingdom shall be established forever before you. Your throne shall be established forever."* [2] Here was promised a king reigning forever, who would be directly descended from King David.

There is no doubt that the Lord Jesus Christ is this promised son of David who would rule on David's throne and in his presence for ever. Admittedly, David's immediate son, Solomon, partially fulfilled the promise, but long after Solomon's death the complete fulfilment was still eagerly anticipated. Isaiah, in words universally applied to Jesus but rarely properly understood, said of the coming son that should be born: *"Of the increase of His government and peace there will be no end, upon the **throne of David and over His kingdom**, to order it and establish it with judgment and justice from that time forward, even forever. The zeal of the LORD of hosts will perform this".* [3] There is overwhelming evidence that the Bible writers taught that one day Jesus would actually reign as king on the earth.

When the angel Gabriel announced to Mary that she would be the mother of Jesus he said that this would be in fulfilment of

---

1. Acts 13.32 **2.** 2 Samuel 7.12–14, 16 **3.** Isaiah 9.7

God's promise to David: *"He will be great, and will be called the Son of the Highest; and the Lord God will give Him the throne of His father David. And he will reign over the house of Jacob forever, and of His kingdom there will be no end."*[1]

Is that what you were taught? Do you expect Jesus to reign on David's restored throne in Jerusalem one day?

God's promise to Abraham

But much earlier, God made a promise concerning Jesus to another Jewish "father": Abraham. He was the ancestor of all the Jewish people. Paul tells us that this promise, although it was made nearly 2000 years before Jesus was born, is in fact nothing less than the gospel: *"And the Scripture, foreseeing that God would justify the Gentiles by faith, **preached the gospel** to Abraham beforehand, saying, 'In you all the nations shall be blessed.'"*[2]

Does God's promise to Abraham fit in with your concept of the Christian gospel?

Let us go back to the earliest days of Christianity and listen to the Apostle Peter preaching in Jerusalem. His clear message was that the Jesus whom the Jews had just crucified had been raised from the dead, had ascended to heaven and was to return to the earth. This was, he said, so that: *"times of refreshing may come from the presence of the Lord, and that he may send Jesus Christ, who was preached to you before, whom heaven must receive until the times of restoration of all things, which God has spoken by the mouth of all his holy prophets since the world began."*[3] Note here that the literal return of Jesus to bring refreshing and blessing to the earth was the central theme of Peter's preaching in the earliest days of Christianity.

---

1. Luke 1.32–33 **2.** Galatians 3.8 **3.** Acts 3.19–21

But Peter does not stop there. He equates this future time of refreshing with God's promise to Abraham made centuries before. He ended his speech by speaking of: *"The covenant which God made with our fathers, saying to Abraham, 'And in your seed all the families of the earth shall be blessed.'"*[1] Don't fail to see the significance of this. All the earth will be blessed when God's promise to Abraham is fulfilled.

We obviously need to go back to Genesis to find out more. (Incidentally, this is why acceptance of the Old Testament is so vital for a genuine Christian.) Abraham was an outstandingly faithful man and because of this God promised him an amazing future. Over Abraham's lifetime God repeated this promise several times.[2] Here are just two of these occasions.

When Abraham had migrated to the land of Canaan (now called Israel), God said to him: *"Lift your eyes now and look from the place where you are – northward, southward, eastward, and westward; for all the land which you see I give to you and your descendants forever."*[3]

On the occasion that Abraham had demonstrated his faith in God by being prepared to sacrifice his son Isaac, God told him: *"Because you have done this thing, and have not withheld your son, your only son – blessing I will bless you, and multiplying I will multiply your descendants as the stars of the heaven and as the sand which is on the seashore; and your descendants shall possess the gate of their enemies. In your seed all the nations of the earth shall be blessed, because you have obeyed my voice."*[4] And this, Paul says, is the gospel that was *"beforehand preached to Abraham"*.[5]

This was a far-reaching promise. Abraham was to have eternal

---

1. Acts 3.25 **2.** Genesis 12.1–3; 12.7; 13.14–16; 22.15–18 **3.** Genesis 13.14–15
4. Genesis 22.16–18 **5.** Galatians 3.8

possession of the land in which he then only wandered. He was also promised a great number of descendants who would be very successful; and in a literal sense this has happened. All Jews have descended from Abraham (although the true descendants of Abraham are something different, as we will see).

But it is the final part of God's promise that is what the Apostle Peter was speaking of: *"In your seed all the nations of the earth shall be blessed".* This word "seed" (meaning "descendant") can be either singular or plural – meaning one individual seed or a lot of seeds. The New Testament tells us which alternative is meant. Quoting this promise to Abraham, Paul told the Galatians: *"The promises were spoken to Abraham and to his seed. Scripture does not say 'and to seeds,' meaning many people, but 'and to your seed', meaning **one person**, who is Christ."*[1]

So, in promising Abraham a very notable single descendant, God was speaking of Jesus. We can now understand why Peter on almost the very first occasion when Christianity was preached referred to this promise.

And what was the blessing that would come through this great seed of Abraham? Peter tells us. After quoting God's words to Abraham *"And in your seed all the families of the earth shall be blessed"*, he then told his audience: *"To you first, God, having raised up his servant Jesus, sent him to bless you, **in turning away every one of you from your iniquities**."*[2] So the blessing God promised to "all the families of the earth" was forgiveness of sins. No wonder that Paul later wrote that this promise to Abraham was in fact the Christian gospel: *"God... preached the gospel to Abraham beforehand, saying, 'In you all*

---

1. Galatians 3.16 NIV   2. Acts 3.25–26

the nations shall be blessed.'" [1]

But this blessing of forgiveness is not automatic. The Christian has to do something in order to share in this blessing. Paul again: *"For as many of you as were baptised into Christ have put on Christ... there is neither Jew nor Greek... for you are all one in Christ Jesus. And if you are Christ's, then you are Abraham's seed, and heirs according to the promise."* [2]

So to receive this blessing of forgiveness a Christian has to "put on Christ" by baptism (more of which later). The baptised person then becomes part of that multitude of "descendants" promised to Abraham, and can receive the forgiveness we all need.

But the future blessing that comes from Abraham's seed is even more extensive. When Jesus returns he will be king over the whole earth. The Bible has many word pictures describing Christ's future rule. Read Psalm 72, which describes the rich worldwide blessings of peace and prosperity of the Kingdom of God under Christ's beneficent rule. The psalm concludes with words that reflect the promise to Abraham: *"His name shall endure forever; his name shall continue as long as the sun. And men shall be blessed in him; all nations shall call him blessed."* [3]

These "covenants of promise" to Abraham and David [4] were the core beliefs of the first Christians. They looked forward to when they would be fulfilled. To them they **were** the gospel.

Do you feel the same about them? Are you part of "Abraham's seed", and an heir according to the promise?

1. Galatians 3.8   2. 3 Galatians 3.27–29   3. Psalm 72.17
4. For a more detailed study of the promises to Abraham and David see *Thine is the Kingdom*, by the present author

Chapter 6
Will Jesus come again?

The return of Jesus to earth is sometimes almost treated as a joke, and "till kingdom come" has passed into common parlance as something that will never happen or is so remote as to be insignificant.

But if, as we have seen earlier, Jesus is to reign on David's throne; if Isaiah's prediction that *"of... his government and peace there will be no end"*[1] will actually happen; and if Abraham is to take eternal possession of the land in which he was once a nomad – then Jesus must come back to earth.

At Christ's ascension to heaven two angels said to the perplexed disciples: *"Men of Galilee, why do you stand gazing up into heaven? This same Jesus, who was taken up from you into heaven, will so come in like manner as you saw him go into heaven."*[2] A multitude of passages in the New Testament show that the return of Jesus was the mainspring of the Christian belief and hope.[3]

Do you, as a Christian, share this hope? Do you *"eagerly wait for the Saviour, the Lord Jesus Christ"*[4] to return from heaven?

Or are you (perish the thought) among those of whom the Apostle Peter wrote: *"Scoffers will come in the last days... saying, 'Where is the promise of His coming? For since the fathers fell asleep, all things continue as they were from the beginning of creation'"?*[5] If you are, then what do you make of these words of your Master: *"Blessed are those servants whom the master, when he comes, will find watching... Therefore you also must be ready, for the Son of Man is coming*

---

1. Isaiah 9.7   2. Acts 1.11   3. Matthew 25.31; Luke 9.26; Luke 21.27; Acts 3.20;
Colossians 3.4; 2 Thessalonians 1.7; 2 Timothy 4.1; Hebrews 9.28; Revelation 22.12
4. Philippians 3.20   5. 2 Peter 3.3–4

at an hour you do not expect." [1]

Why is Christ coming back?

*   To be a king that rules over the whole world:

"The kingdoms of this world have become the kingdoms of our Lord and of His Christ, and He shall reign forever and ever." [2] *"When the Son of Man comes in His glory, and all the holy angels with Him, then He will sit on the throne of His glory. All the nations will be gathered before Him."* [3]

*   To bless all nations with peace and security:

"Behold, a king will reign in righteousness, and princes will rule with justice… The work of righteousness will be peace, and the effect of righteousness, quietness and assurance forever." [4] *"They shall beat their swords into plowshares, and their spears into pruning hooks; nation shall not lift up sword against nation, neither shall they learn war anymore."* [5]

*   To reward his friends:

"For the Son of Man will come in the glory of His Father with His angels, and then He will reward each according to his works." [6] *"So an entrance will be supplied to you abundantly into the everlasting kingdom of our Lord and Savior Jesus Christ."* [7] *"Everyone who sees the Son and believes in him may have everlasting life; and I will raise him up at the last day."* [8]

*   To be the world's judge.

Most Christians today concentrate on the benign, loveable aspects of the character of Jesus – the "Gentle Jesus meek and mild" of the children's hymn. And indeed that is an aspect of his personality that is most important and most comforting to his

---

1. Luke 12.37, 40 **2.** Revelation 11.15 **3.** Matthew 25.31–32 **4.** Isaiah 32.1, 17
5. Isaiah 2.4 **6.** Matthew 16.27 **7.** 2 Peter 1.11 **8.** John 6.40

followers. But there is another aspect that is equally prominent in the divine record, which is rarely mentioned by Christians today. Jesus, as well as being the embodiment of love, is a just judge, and is portrayed as punishing offenders at his return to earth.

If you continue reading from the passage we have just quoted from Luke you will find this other side of Christ's character. Speaking of some who are unprepared for his return Jesus continues: *"The master of that servant will come on a day when he is not looking for him, and at an hour when he is not aware, and will cut him in two and appoint him his portion with the unbelievers."*[1]

Not only unfaithful individuals, but also all organised opposition to him will be violently destroyed. Just consider the following references and see if they fit in with your concept of Jesus.

- *"His winnowing fan is in His hand, and He will thoroughly clean out His threshing floor, and gather His wheat into the barn; but He will burn up the chaff with unquenchable fire."*[2]

- *"You who are troubled rest with us when the Lord Jesus is revealed from heaven with his mighty angels, in flaming fire taking vengeance on those who do not know God, and on those who do not obey the gospel of our Lord Jesus Christ."*[3]

- *"And then the lawless one will be revealed, whom the Lord will consume with the breath of His mouth and destroy with the brightness of His coming."*[4]

- *"Now I saw heaven opened, and behold, a white horse. And He who sat on him was called Faithful and True, and in righteousness he judges and makes war... Now out of his*

---

1. Luke 12.46 **2.** Matthew 3.12 **3.** 2 Thessalonians 1.7–8 **4.** 2 Thessalonians 2.8

mouth goes a sharp sword, that with it He should strike the nations. And he himself will rule them with a rod of iron. He himself treads the winepress of the fierceness and wrath of Almighty God."[1]

With all this absolutely plain teaching about Christ's future role, and its vast implication for us, and the world at large, are you happy that among the majority of Christians today there is little expectation of his return?

---

1. Revelation 19.11, 15

Chapter 7

Is the doctrine of the Trinity a biblical concept?

Now we come to the really big challenge – the Trinity.[1] The vast majority of Christians believe that God is composed of three persons, all co-equal and co-eternal. This is considered to be so basic to Christianity that any who deny this doctrine are by definition not Christian. For example, one website says of the Trinity: "Belief in it defines a Christian. It is almost universally held in Trinitarian Christianity, that denial of the Trinity is a renunciation of Christianity and salvation."

On the other hand, some recognise that the earliest Christians knew nothing of the doctrine. In outlining the development of the doctrine of the Trinity since New Testament times, William Rusch, an American Christian theologian, writes in his book *The Trinitarian Controversy* that some: "have seen the developments [of the doctrine of the Trinity] traced in this volume as *a capitulation of the biblical revelation to a foreign system from which Christianity has still not yet escaped.*"[2]

So we clearly need to have an impartial look into this basic belief. Is it, to use Rusch's words, "biblical revelation" or an imported "foreign system"?

Let's start by defining the doctrine of the Trinity as outlined in church creeds today.

The first attempt to formally define it was in the year 325, at the Council of Nicea, nearly 300 years after Christianity was first preached. For our purpose the relevant points of this Nicene

---

1. For a more complete examination of the field covered in this chapter see *The Trinity – True or False* by J.H. Broughton and P.J. Southgate, available from the Dawn Book Supply **2.** William Rusch, p. 27; Fortress Press, Philadelphia, 1980 (italics added)

Creed are:

"We believe in one God the Father Almighty, Maker of heaven and earth, and of all things visible and invisible. And in one Lord Jesus Christ, the only-begotten Son of God, begotten of the Father before all worlds, God of God, Light of Light, Very God of Very God, begotten, not made, being of one substance with the Father by whom all things were made... And we believe in the Holy Spirit, the Lord and Giver of Life, who proceedeth from the Father, who with the Father and the Son together is worshipped and glorified, who spoke by the prophets."

About 200 years later the views were elaborated in the Athanasian Creed. This is very long and repetitive, but here is a sample of its main teaching:

"We worship one God in trinity, and trinity in unity; neither confounding the persons; nor dividing the substance. For there is one person of the Father: another of the Son: another of the Holy Spirit. But the Godhead of the Father, and of the Son, and of the Holy Spirit is all one: the glory equal, the majesty co-eternal... The Father is eternal: the Son eternal: the Holy Spirit eternal. And yet there are not three eternals; but one eternal."

The doctrine of the Trinity – undisputed facts

In considering the trinitarian doctrine it is helpful to first establish some indisputable facts.

1. It is not taught in the Bible

It may surprise you to learn that it has always been recognised that none of the significant phrases in either of these creeds, or even the ideas they express, can be found anywhere in the Bible, as the following quotations show, all of which are from avowed Christians:

- John Milton (author of *Paradise Lost*, 1608–1674): "For my part I adhere to the Holy Scriptures alone, I follow no other heresy or sect. If, therefore, the Father be the God of Christ, and the same be our God, and if there be none other God but one, there can be no God beside the Father."[1] Commenting on this, another writer says: "John Locke and Isaac Newton, with Milton the three greatest names of the period (c.1650), could not find Trinitarianism in the Bible."[2]

• George Smallridge (Bishop of Bristol, 1663–1710): "It must be owned, that the doctrine of the Trinity as it is proposed in our Articles, our Liturgy, our Creeds, is not in so many words taught us in the Holy Scriptures. What we profess in our prayers we nowhere read in Scripture, that the one God, the one Lord, is not only one person, but three persons in one substance. There is no such text as this, 'That the Unity in Trinity, and the Trinity in Unity is to be worshipped'. No one of the inspired writers hath expressly affirmed, that in the Trinity none is afore or after other, none is greater or less than another."[3]

• Johann Neander (German theologian and Church historian, 1789–1850): "The Doctrine of the Trinity does not, it appears to me, belong strictly to the fundamentals of the Christian faith; as it appears from the fact that it is explicitly set forth in no one particular passage of the New Testament; for the only one in which this is done, the passage relating to the three that bear record [1 John 5.7] is undoubtedly spurious, and in its ungenuine shape testifies to the fact."[4]

• Dr Joseph Priestly (1871): "Why was not the doctrine of the *Trinity* taught as explicitly, and in as definite a manner, in the New Testament at least, as the doctrine of the divine *Unity* is taught in both the Old and New Testaments, if it be a

---

1. Quoted by H. Stannus: *A history of the Trinity in the Early Church*. Christian Life Publishing, London
2. Christopher Mill, *Milton and the English Revelation*; pp. 286, 296
3. *Sixty Sermons*, No. xxxiii, p. 343 4. *History of Christian Religion*, vol. ii p. 286

truth? And why is the doctrine of the *Unity* always delivered in so unguarded a manner and without any exception made in favour of the Trinity, to prevent any mistake with respect to it?"[1]

- Thomas Mozeley (the brother-in-law of the famous nineteenth-century Cardinal Newman): "I ask with all humbleness where the idea of Threeness is expressed in the New Testament with a doctrinal sense and force? Where is the Triune God held up to be worshipped, loved and obeyed? Where is He preached and proclaimed in that threefold Character? ... Certainly not in Scripture do we find the expression 'God the Son', or 'God the Holy Ghost'. Whenever I pronounce the name of God, simply and first, I mean God the Father, and I cannot help meaning that, if I mean anything."[2]

- Dr W. Matthews (Dean of St Paul's Cathedral,1940): "It must be admitted by everyone who has the rudiments of an historical sense that the doctrine of the Trinity, as a doctrine, formed no part of the original message. St Paul knew it not, and would have been unable to understand the meaning of the terms used in the theological formula on which the Church ultimately agreed."[3]

- *Encyclopedia of Religion* (1987): "Theologians today are in agreement that the Hebrew Bible does not contain a doctrine of the Trinity. Further, theologians agree that the New Testament also does not contain an explicit doctrine of the trinity nor does the New Testament contain the technical language of later doctrine."[4]

Don't you think that testimonies such as these should make us

1. *A History of the Corruptions of Christianity*. The British and Foreign Unitarian Association, London, 1871   2. *Reminiscences of the Oriel College and the Oxford Movement*   3. *God in Christian Thought and Experience*   4. Article: *Trinity*

hesitate before saying that the Trinity is a basic doctrine that defines Christianity and that salvation is impossible without it?

2. It formed no part of the early Christian beliefs

This increasing evidence that the Trinity is not a Bible doctrine is strengthened on considering the beliefs of the earliest Christians and subsequent history. Again, the following are indisputable facts.

It was not an original Christian doctrine, but gradually developed over a period of 300 years. As a modern writer says: "In order to understand the doctrine of the Trinity it is necessary to understand that the doctrine is a *development*, and why it developed... It is a waste of time to attempt to read Trinitarian doctrine directly off the pages of the New Testament."[1]

For several years virtually all the converts to Christianity were Jews, who were (as are the Jews today) fanatical about the unity of God. Their basic text was: *"Hear, O Israel: The LORD our God, the LORD is one."*[2] This is repeated many times throughout the Old Testament: *"For I am God, and there is no other; I am God, and there is none like me."*[3]

If, therefore, the Apostles were preaching the Trinity, the first major obstacle would be to convince their Jewish audience that God was no longer one person but three. They would have needed to spell out quite clearly the arguments in support of this new concept, had it existed. Yet, as trinitarians freely acknowledge, there is no trace of such confrontation or discussion in the early church. As a prominent nineteenth-century Christian theologian observed: "The doctrine, then, is never defended in the New Testament, though unquestionably it would have been the main object of attack, and the main

---

1. A & R Hanson: *Reasonable Belief. A survey of the Christian Faith*, p 170, 1980, italics added 2. Deuteronomy 6.4 3. Isaiah 46.9

difficulty in the Christian system. It is never explained, though no doctrine could have been so much in need of explanation… And still more, this doctrine is never insisted upon as a necessary article of faith; though it is now represented by its defenders as lying at the foundation of Christianity."[1]

To this can be added the words of Cardinal Newman, the prominent nineteenth-century theologian recently beatified by the Pope, who admitted that the Trinity was not believed in the early church. He says that although some other doctrines were "consistently and uniformly confessed by the Primitive Church… But it surely is otherwise with the Catholic doctrine of the Trinity. I do not see in what sense it can be said that there is a consensus of primitive [Church authorities] in its favour."[2]

3. It was a gradual development over more than 300 years

History describes that although it clearly was not an original tenet of the Christian faith, the teaching of the relationship between God and Jesus gradually changed over the first few centuries of the Christian era. The importation of Greek philosophical ideas by the early Christian "fathers" and the desire to make Christianity more palatable to the wider pagan community very slowly modified the original belief. Three hundred years of discussion (indeed confrontation, for the changes were strongly resisted in some quarters) resulted in the formal statement of the Trinity as it is taught today.

This process was, according to one historian, not a straightforward and "unerring homing towards the truth", but "a process of trial and error, almost hit and miss".[3] The deity of the Holy Spirit was not considered or addressed for another 56 years after the Nicene creed was formulated. In 381, at the Council of Constantinople, the Holy Spirit was given equal

1. Andrews Norton (1833). *A Statement of Reasons For Not Believing The Doctrines of Trinitarians, Concerning The Nature of God and The Person of Christ*
2. Cardinal John Henry Newman (1845) *An Essay on the Development of Christian Doctrine*. 2nd edition (London: J. Toovey, 1846), pp. 14–18, 40–42.
3. A & R Hanson: *Reasonable Belief. A survey of the Christian Faith*, p.171, 1980

status with Father and Son. The final definition of the doctrine was thus agreed upon and then made binding on all Christians. This obligation to believe in the Trinity was not imposed by the church leaders of the day, but by the decree of the Roman Emperor, who threatened severe sanctions for non-compliance.[1]

The ecclesiastical historian Mosheim, when commenting on the gradual doctrinal changes in the first few centuries, says: "Thus it was with the doctrine of Christ, his person and natures... For that *devout and venerable simplicity of the first ages of the church*, which made men believe when God speaks, and obey when he commands, was thought by the chief doctors of this age [sixth century] to be *only fit for clowns*."[2]

What is your view? Do you also consider the beliefs of the early Christians "only fit for clowns"?

But with the coming of the Reformation, when the Bible had been translated into common languages for all to read, it is significant that the first doctrine to be challenged was that of the Trinity, and some of those who queried it paid with their lives – even at the hands of their fellow Christians.[3]

At the beginning of this section we quoted William Rusch, who said that the development of the doctrine of the Trinity was: "a capitulation of the biblical revelation to a foreign system from which Christianity has still not yet escaped".[4]

Are you still as sure about the Trinity as you were?

Passages showing Christ's relationship to his Father

So much for history and the opinions of leading Christians. But more importantly, what does the Bible itself say? Here are some more facts, taken from Scripture itself.

---

1. Theodosius: *Epsicopi tradi.*, July 381   2. J.L. Mosheim, D.D. *Ecclesiastical History.* Book II, Cent vi, ch. 3. London,1863; italics added   3. For example, Michael Servetus 1511–1553, who was burnt at the stake for his denial of the Trinity; William Penn the founder of the Quaker movement, and many others
4. W. Rusch, p. 27; Fortress Press, Philadelphia, 1980, italics added

In answer to a question about the greatest commandment, Jesus replied: *"The first of all the commandments is: 'Hear, O Israel, the LORD our God, the LORD is one.'"*[1] If God was three in one what an excellent opportunity for explanation was missed.

Jesus repeatedly stated his subordination to his Father: *"My Father is greater than I"*;[2] *"The Son can do nothing of himself"*;[3] *My Father… is greater than all"*.[4] The Apostle Paul confirms this relationship still applied in his day (when Jesus was in heaven in the presence of the Father): *"The head of Christ is God"*.[5] He also says that in the future, *"when all things are made subject to him, then the Son himself will also be subject to him* [i.e. God] *who put all things under him"*.[6] So Jesus is subordinate to the Father and will be in all future ages.

Surely, even just one of these statements should make us pause for thought. But when the same ideas are repeated time and again, it is difficult to believe that Scripture teaches the co-equality of Father and Son.

Scripture also says that Jesus was "sent" by God, and that there was a possible conflict of wills, implying subordination. Had he been so inclined, Jesus could have asserted a different view, implying a separate personality: *"I do not seek my own will but the will of the Father who sent me."*[7] *"I do nothing of myself; but as My Father taught me, I speak these things."*[8]

Further, Jesus, even after his resurrection and glorification, still describes his Father as "my God". He said to the disciples: *"I am ascending to **my Father** and your Father, and to **my God** and your God."*[9] Later he uses the same terms in the book of Revelation: *"I will make him a pillar in the temple of **my God**…*

---

1. Mark 12.29   2. John 14.28   3. John 5.19, 30   4. John 10.29
5. 1 Corinthians 11.3   6. 1 Corinthians 15.28   7. John 5.30   8. John 8.28
9. John 20.17

*I will write on him the name of **my God** and the name of the city of **my God**, the New Jerusalem."*[1]

So I ask: does the Bible really teach the equality of Father and Son?

But what about...?

I'm sure that after reading so far many of my readers will have been fidgeting in their seats – if not jumping out of them – impatient to refer me to the Bible passages that they feel amply support the doctrine of the Trinity. But please ask yourself as we now proceed: "If I did not have the Trinity **already in mind** would I have deduced it from any passage that apparently supports the idea?"

At one time a passage from the letter of John was always quoted as proof: *"For there are three that bear record in heaven, the Father, the Word, and the Holy Ghost: and these three are one."*[2]

For centuries this was the proof text to demonstrate the Trinity, but now it is never mentioned in its support. Why? Because it is widely recognised that this was a fraudulent addition, dating from about the fifth century. Most modern versions omit this reference, often without even a word of explanation. So, whilst it cannot now be used in support of the doctrine, it makes one ask that if the Bible clearly taught the doctrine elsewhere in its pages, why did some scheming copyist feel the need to insert it?

"But", you might say, "there are many other passages that imply the Trinity even if they do not actually spell it out." Well, let's look at some.

But before that I would like to repeat something I said on

---

1. Revelation 3.12   **2.** 1 John 5.7

page 12. If one comes to the Bible with preconceived ideas it is sometimes possible to find a few verses that appear to support them. But that is entirely different from coming to the Bible with an open mind to learn what it really teaches. This is particularly true of the Trinity, as the following examples will show.

"I and my Father are one"[1]

The saying: "A quotation without a context is a pretext", applies here. Read the verses prior to this phrase to see what Jesus is really saying. He is referring to the safety of "his sheep", and gives them two guarantees of protection. The first is in his own ability and love: *"neither shall anyone snatch them out of my hand"* (v. 28). But in addition they have the even greater protection afforded by his Father: *"My Father, who has given them to me, is greater than all; and no one is able to snatch them out of my Father's hand"* (v. 29). So here is a double guarantee: both God and Jesus will protect true Christians. And in this intention and ability to protect the sheep Jesus and his Father are united: *"I and my Father are one"*. This is obviously Christ's meaning. Jesus and his Father are as one in their desire and ability to care for those who believe. Thus, his words have no trinitarian overtones. And note that even in this regularly quoted passage the Trinity is excluded by Christ's express statement that his Father is the greater.

"Before Abraham was, I AM"[2]

Trinitarians claim that here Jesus is applying to himself the name by which God revealed Himself to Moses at the burning bush: *"And God said to Moses, 'I AM WHO I AM.' And he said, 'Thus you shall say to the children of Israel, "I AM has sent me to you".'"*[3] In recent Bible versions the trinitarian bias of the

---

1. John 10.30 **2.** John 8.58 **3.** Exodus 3.14

translators is shown by capitalising the "I AM", but, as stated earlier,[1] there is no such capitalisation in the original manuscripts. Translating "I am" in this way is simply an attempt to foist the translator's personal predilections on the readers.

The phrase "I am" is a translation of two common Greek words *ego eimi*, which occur frequently in the New Testament. It simply means "I am the one" and in almost every place it occurs it is translated as "I am he". Because the "he" does not occur in the Greek, on Bible translations it is usually added in italics to make the sense clear – as in all other instances but this one.

There are examples of this phrase in the very same chapter in John, which obviously have no trinitarian connotation: *"If you do not believe that I am he, you will die in your sins"; "When you lift up the Son of Man, then you will know that I am he, and that I do nothing of myself".*[2] You might ask why the translators did not use capital letters for "I am he" in these cases.

Jesus used similar language when he claimed his Messiahship to the woman of Samaria. She said: *"'I know that Messiah is coming' (who is called Christ). 'When he comes, he will tell us all things.' Jesus said to her, 'I who speak to you am he.'"*[3] Thus, when Jesus was asked if he was the Messiah he simply replied, "Yes, I am the one."

What, then, was Jesus meaning by saying that before Abraham existed: "I am he"? He was simply stating that he was the promised Messiah – the one promised to Abraham (see page 37); and says that with the eye of faith that patriarch looked forward with joy to the arrival of his notable descendant.[4]

"The Word made flesh"

This passage has been in my consciousness for over 70 years,

---

1. Page 20 **2.** John 8.24, 28 **3.** John 4.25–26. For other clearly non-trinitarian implications of *eigo eimi* see Luke 21.8; John 9.9; 13.19; 18.5; 18.8; Acts 10.21; Revelation 1.18; 2.23 **4.** John 8.56

ever since as a young schoolboy I queried the Trinity with my Religious Instruction master. He turned me to John 1.1: *"In the beginning was the Word, and the Word was with God, and the Word was God. He was in the beginning with God. All things were made through Him."*[1] He said that "the Word" meant Jesus, as shown by verse 14: *"And the Word became flesh and dwelt among us, and we beheld his glory, the glory as of the only begotten of the Father, full of grace and truth."* "There you are," he commented, "Jesus, the Word, existed from the beginning and then took on human flesh at his birth." My inexperience prevented any disputing this interpretation, but if he were with me now I would make the following observations:

- We must not interpret John's writings in a way that contradicts the clear teaching of other Scripture. John had a unique form of expression that often had a different "under the surface" meaning.

- I would point out that "Word" is a translation of the common Greek word *logos* and there is nothing to indicate that it needs a capital letter.

- Further, in the eminent Greek scholar Tyndale's translation of the New Testament (the basis for our King James version) *logos* is correctly translated as "it" rather than "him": *"In the beginning was that word, and that word was with God: and God was that word. The same was in the beginning with God. All things were made by it, and without it, was made nothing that was made. In it was life…"*[2] This rendering was also adopted in the Geneva Bible of 1560 (the commonly used version in Elizabethan and Puritan times) and the Bishop's Bible of 1568, both of which also give no hint of personality attached to "the word". It was only when the

---

1. John 1.1–3   2. John 1.1-4, Tyndale 1535

bishops convened to produce the 1611 King James Version that their trinitarian prejudices turned Tyndale's "it" into "him".

Sorry, but we need to introduce a bit of Greek here – otherwise we cannot get just what John meant by "word". As just mentioned it is the Greek word *logos* – from which we derive many of our everyday words. For example, "biology" is literally the "word" (*logos*) about "life" (*bios*). A Greek lexicon defines *logos* as meaning: "The expression of thought (a) as embodying a conception or idea; (b) a saying or statement".[1] It does not mean simply a group of letters, as "a word" indicates today.

So let's put these first-century meanings (as given by the lexicon) into John's opening verses: "In the beginning was the **idea,** and the **idea** was with God, and the **idea** was God. This **conception** was in the beginning with God. All things were made through it." Does that now convey, let alone demand, the existence of an additional person who was present at the beginning?

Isn't John actually saying that at the beginning God had a plan – a plan that was inseparable from Him. And that plan was expressed in His word – as He says through Isaiah: *"So shall my word be that goes forth from my mouth; it shall not return to me void... and it shall prosper in the thing for which I sent it."*[2] The "word" is the thoughts and purposes of God in action.

Right from the beginning God had a plan for the earth and mankind – a plan that was inseparable from Himself – a plan for which He created the world – a plan that necessitated the coming of a saviour. And, as John goes on to say, that plan, that word, materialised in the person of Jesus: *"And the word became flesh and dwelt among us, and we beheld his glory, the*

---

1. *Vines Expository Dictionary of New Testament Words;* Oliphants Ltd, 1940
2. Isaiah 55.11

glory as of the only begotten of the Father, full of grace and truth."[1] To quote William Barclay, the much-respected Bible scholar, "We might well translate John's words, 'The mind of God became a man.'"[2] So John is saying that at the coming of Jesus, God's age-old plan was being put into effect. He was not implying that Jesus was God or had personally existed from before the creation.

"I have come down from heaven"[3]

Jesus often used language like this, which, taken at face value, suggests that he had a previous existence in heaven. But, along with many of Christ's words recorded only by John, a literal interpretation is excluded by other Scripture.

In this instance, Jesus was comparing his teaching with the manna sent by God from heaven at the Exodus that sustained Israel in the wilderness.[4] He said that unlike Moses, who gave them literal food from heaven, God was now giving the "true bread from heaven" – Jesus himself. Of this he said: *"This is the bread which comes down from heaven, that one may eat of it and not die."*[5] So Jesus was not indicating that he had literally come down from heaven, but that he was the counterpart of the heaven-sent manna, which if spiritually "eaten" brings eternal life.

There are several other references, exclusive to John, where Jesus appears to say that he was in heaven previous to his life on earth.[6]

The fact that all these allusions to Christ coming down from heaven are found only in the gospel record of John should make us pause. Did the other New Testament writers know of the pre-existence of Christ in heaven but did not mention it?

---

1. John 1.14 2. W. Barclay, *The Gospel of John*, p. xxii 3. John 6.38 4. Exodus 16
5. John 6.50 6. John 3.13; 3.31; 6.38; 8.32; 16.28; 17.5

Or could it be that John had a distinctive way of looking at the words of Jesus that bids us look beneath their apparent meaning?

Many of Christ's sayings recorded by John were not intended to be taken literally, although sometimes his hearers did just that. When Jesus told Nicodemus that he needed to be "born anew", he first took a literal interpretation: *"How can a man be born when he is old?"*[1] When Jesus said to the Jewish leaders: *"You are from beneath; I am from above,"*[2] he was obviously using figurative language, for they did not come from under the ground. He later admitted that such figurative language was his practice.[3]

Peter clearly explains the true situation – that prior to his birth Jesus existed in the mind of God, and God's intention regarding him was not put into effect until his birth actually took place: *"He indeed was **foreordained** before the foundation of the world, but was **manifest** in these last times for you."*[4]

"In the form of God" [5]

There is another passage to which trinitarians invariably turn in support of their belief in the deity of Jesus. It is one that superficially supports the doctrine, especially if someone comes to it with the Trinity already in mind. The key passage speaks of Jesus who, *"being in the form of God, did not consider it robbery to be equal with God, but made himself of no reputation, taking the form of a bondservant, and coming in the likeness of men".*[6]

It is claimed that this describes the incarnation of Jesus, who having existed in heaven with God divested himself of his divinity and became a man.

---

1. John 3.4   **2.** John 8.23   **3.** John 16.25   **4.** 1 Peter 1.20   **5.** Philippians 2.3–11
6. Philippians 2.6–7

We need to ask some questions about this. Paul is trying to impress on his readers the need for them to copy the humility of Christ. The previous verse reads: *"Let this mind be in you which was also in Christ Jesus."* So we ask, how could the Philippians copy Christ in the particular way that Paul was suggesting? Could they also come down from heaven and become man? As a professor of divinity once said: "Paul is begging the Philippians to cease from dissension and to act with humility towards each other... It is asked whether it would be quite natural for him to enforce these simple moral lessons by incidental reference (and the only reference that he ever makes) to the vast problem of the mode of the incarnation."[1]

Or another scholar: "Looking afresh at Philippians chapter 2, we must ask the question whether Paul in these verses has really made what would be his only allusion to Jesus' having been alive before his birth. The context of his remarks shows him to be urging the saints to be humble. It is often asked whether it is in any way probable that he would enforce the lesson by asking his readers to adopt the frame of mind of one who, having been eternally God, made the decision to become man."[2]

True. Would it not have been more appropriate for Paul to have pointed to the inspiring example of Christ's humility and self-sacrifice in his **human** life than in a previous heavenly one?

One further point of many that we could make: Paul goes on to say that as a result of Christ's humility and obedience even to death: *"God also has highly exalted Him and given Him the name which is above every name."*[3] Several points arise here: (1) Jesus was exalted as a result of his humility, therefore he could not have previously been divine; (2) Jesus was then

---

1. A.H. McNeile, *New Testament Teaching in the Light of St Paul's*, 1923, pp.65–66
2. A. Buzzard, *Who is Jesus?* p. 20   3. Philippians 2.9

given "the name" above every name, so clearly he did not possess that divine name earlier; and (3) Christ's exaltation was "to the glory of God the Father", implying the lesser status of the Son.

The greatness of Jesus

But in all the foregoing, which shows that Jesus was not a component of a divine Trinity and that he has a lesser status, we certainly do not demean the person, the life, the works and the achievements of our Saviour. He was absolutely unique, the *"express image"*[1] of the Father, and spiritually he resided *"in the bosom of the Father"*.[2] All men should therefore *"honour the Son just as they honour the Father"*.[3] He was the Word of God revealed to us, expressing to mankind God's attributes, thoughts, example and purpose. He will become King of Kings and Lord of Lords[4] and is worthy of all the praise, adoration and honour that poor mortals can bestow.[5] Next to God he is the greatest being in the universe.

But he is not God in the trinitarian sense.

---

1. Hebrews 1.3.   2. John 1.18   3. John 5.23   4. Revelation 19.16
5. Revelation 5.12

Chapter 8
Is baptism necessary?

As a professing Christian, how do you respond to the question, "Have you been baptised?" In my experience most would say, "Yes, I have", but some would say, "No, for I don't feel baptism is essential for my ultimate salvation."

To the first group, dare I put another question: "What form did your baptism take, and when did it happen?" Many, possibly the majority, would reply, "I was given Christian baptism as a baby and thus became a member of Christ's church." This ceremony, commonly called "christening", has an extremely long tradition – as evidenced by the baptismal fonts in churches dating from very ancient times to the present day.

But how does it square with Bible teaching and the very earliest Christian practice?

In fact there is not the slightest evidence for the current practice of christening in the Bible. Originally, biblical baptism was only given to a person who had demonstrated belief in the gospel and had confessed that faith, which is clearly not possible for a young infant. This was followed by a complete immersion in water and the resolve to adopt a reformed life.

After his resurrection Jesus commissioned his disciples to preach the gospel throughout the world, saying that: *"He who believes and is baptized will be saved; but he who does not believe will be condemned."*[1]

The Apostles did as Jesus commanded and it is significant that in the Acts of the Apostles every instance of conversion to the

---

1. Mark 16.16; also Matthew 28.19

new faith, as a result of their preaching, is followed by the record of that convert's baptism. For example, on the very first occasion that Christianity was preached to the world on the day of Pentecost, the hearer's response was: *"'Men and brethren, what shall we do?' Then Peter said to them, 'Repent, and let every one of you be baptized in the name of Jesus Christ for the remission of sins.'"*[1]

In his letter written later, the Apostle Peter says that baptism *"saves us"*.[2] Christian doctrine is all about "saving" and forgiveness of sins; so how can some say that baptism is unnecessary?

As to the mode of baptism, there is absolutely no doubt that it was by complete immersion in water. Acts records that after an Ethiopian eunuch's confession of faith in Jesus, *"both Philip and the eunuch **went down into** the water, and he baptized him"*.[3] The word "baptise" even demands complete immersion. It is derived from a Greek word once used in the dyeing process. Cloth had to be completely submerged in the liquid dye in order to be changed to the new colour – merely sprinkling dye on the cloth was obviously useless.

In Romans 6 the Apostle Paul describes that at baptism, when a believer is buried in water, he or she undergoes in figure what Jesus did in fact – death, burial and resurrection to a new life: *"Do you not know that as many of us as were baptized into Christ Jesus were baptized into His death? Therefore we were buried with Him through baptism into death, that just as Christ was raised from the dead by the glory of the Father, even so we also should walk in newness of life."*[4]

So I repeat, it is absolutely certain that the original Christian

---

1. Acts 2.37–38   **2.** 1 Peter 3.21   **3.** Acts 8.38   **4.** Romans 6.3–4

baptism was a confession of belief in Christ, followed by immersion in water. It had to be by a believing adult.

How and why did it change to what is the current practice in many if not most Christian societies? I suspect that the introduction of the belief that all humans had an immortal soul began to put some in a quandary. What would happen to the soul of a poor innocent child who died?

So, soon after the Apostles departed from the scene, and despite the fact that baptism had until then been confined to those who could believe the gospel, pressure was put on the church to ensure that by baptism such infants would be saved. But this originally met with opposition from prominent Christians such as Tertullian (AD 150–225). Speaking of new converts he wrote: "Let them come when they grow up – let them come when they learn; let them become Christians when they are able to know Christ; why should this innocent age hasten to the remission of sins."[1]

But as time went by, infant christening was substituted for immersion, with the sanction of the established church. A well-known Victorian theologian, Dean Stanley, described the change as a "triumph of common sense and convenience over the bondage of form and custom".[2]

Do you, as a follower of Jesus, agree with the Dean?

Sorry to put it bluntly, but if this rite of baptism can be so much changed, how many other of God's specific commands are some Christians prepared to alter under the guise of "common sense and convenience" or "keeping up with the times"? Look around and you might see more examples than you expect.

---

1. Neander's *Church History* chapter 3: "At the beginning of the third century, religious declension had considerably advanced. No one will now be surprised at hearing that an attempt was made to extend the administration of baptism in an unwarrantable manner. It is referred to by Tertullian in his tract, *'De Baptismo'* in terms of strong disapproval." 2. *The Nineteenth Century Review,* October 1879

Chapter 9
Are you ready for Christ's return?

We demonstrated earlier[1] that the return of Jesus to fulfil the "promises made to the fathers" by setting up the Kingdom of God was a central theme of original Christian teaching. But over the long ages since, although it is accepted in theory, it has receded into the background, so that it has no practical effect on the lives and expectations of many individual Christians or the church as a whole.

Yet the teaching of Jesus is crystal clear. He will come back – taking the world by surprise, and we need to be ready for it. It will be as sudden as on past occasions of divine intervention: *"For as in the days before the flood, they were eating and drinking, marrying and giving in marriage, until the day that Noah entered the ark, and did not know until the flood came and took them all away, so also will the coming of the Son of Man be."*[2]

To use another analogy, his return to earth will be as unexpected as the intrusion of a burglar: *"For you yourselves know perfectly that the day of the Lord so comes as a thief in the night."*[3] Hence, Jesus gives this advice: *"Watch therefore... But know this, that if the master of the house had known what hour the thief would come, he would have watched and not allowed his house to be broken into. Therefore you also be ready, for the Son of Man is coming at an hour you do not expect."*[4]

Can you fit this aspect of Christ's teaching into your daily life? Is this thought continually in the back of your mind: "Jesus may come today"?

---

1. Chapters 5 and 6   **2.** Matthew 24.38–39   **3.** 1 Thessalonians 5.2
4. Matthew 24.42–44

Jesus the judge

When Jesus returns it will not be as the benign and gentle Jesus of the children's hymn. He is coming initially as a judge – of individuals and then of the world at large. Jesus said that at his return, when the resurrection has taken place and when he *"sits on the throne of his glory"*, he will divide people into two classes on the basis of the life they have lived. The faithful will be directed to the right of his throne and will hear his words of approval: *"Come, you blessed of My Father, inherit the kingdom prepared for you from the foundation of the world"*, and be given eternal life.[1]

This tribunal and the need for Christians to be prepared for it is repeatedly emphasised in the New Testament. The Apostle Paul often refers to it. *"For we shall all stand before the judgment seat of Christ"*,[2] is just one example.

And what will be the basis for acceptance at this tribunal? *"If you love me keep my commands"*, said Jesus.[3] In his so-called "Sermon on the Mount" Jesus gives details of how he expects his followers to behave. He ends his discourse by saying that those who hear and do what he says will be like a house impregnable to flood and disaster, whilst the house of those who disregard his commands will perish.[4] A very sobering thought.

So there is no doubt that what the Christian does in this life will determine the result of that tribunal. Many other passages of Scripture clearly teach this: *"For we must all appear before the judgment seat of Christ, that each one may receive the things done in the body, according to what he has done, whether good or bad."*[5] The final message of Jesus to his followers reaffirms

---

1. Matthew 25.34, 46   2. Romans 14.10; also 2 Corinthians 5.10; 2 Timothy 4.1
3. John 14.15   4. Matthew chapters 5–7   5. 2 Corinthians 5.10

this: *"And behold, I am coming quickly, and my reward is with me, to give to every one according to his work."*[1] And the "work" of each one has been recorded in a figurative book that will form the basis of the verdict: *"And I saw the dead, small and great, standing before God, and books were opened. And another book was opened, which is the Book of Life. And the dead were judged according to their works, by the things which were written in the books."*[2]

What are the "works" that will enable our judge to accept us? Without entering into the "works" versus "faith" controversy that has beset theologians over many years, we can bring some Bible teaching to bear. Faith in what Jesus achieved is itself a "work". In answer to a question: *"'What shall we do, that we may work the works of God?' Jesus answered and said to them, 'This is the work of God, that you believe in Him whom He sent.'"*[3] Paul commended the Thessalonians for three things: their *"work of faith, labour of love, and patience of hope"*.[4] The Christian's work also includes helping others: *"For God is not unjust to forget your work and labour of love… in that you have ministered to the saints."*[5] Jesus is depicted as saying at his judgement seat to those who "will go into eternal life": *"Assuredly, I say to you, inasmuch as you did it to one of the least of these my brethren, you did it to me."*[6] In that same chapter Jesus praises the diligent servant who had used the talents (abilities) his master had given him, and promises a reward as a result: *"His lord said to him, 'Well done, good and faithful servant; you were faithful over a few things, I will make you ruler over many things. Enter into the joy of your lord.'"* Whereas the lazy servant was *"cast into… outer darkness"*.[7]

It seems, therefore, that both faith and action will determine the

---

1. Revelation 22.12; see also Matthew 16.27   2. Revelation 20.12
3. John 6.29   4. 1 Thessalonians 1.3   5. Hebrews 6.10   6. Matthew 25.46, 40
7. Matthew 25.21, 30

Christian's outcome. But overriding all will be the love and forgiveness of our judge and his earnest desire to bring his true followers into his Kingdom: *"Do not fear, little flock, for it is your Father's good pleasure to give you the kingdom."*[1] Complete forgiveness will be willingly given to those who have striven to be faithful.

Judgements on an evil world

But for the world at large there are ominous Bible predictions about the return of Jesus that few Christians seem to take into consideration. Earlier we quoted from Daniel chapter 2, which describes the changeover on earth from the kingdom of men (the systems in place today) to the Kingdom of God.[2] The kingdom of men is depicted by a huge statue, which came tumbling down in pieces when a stone struck it on its feet. Then all those fallen pieces were: *"crushed together, and became like chaff from the summer threshing floors; the wind carried them away so that no trace of them was found. And the stone that struck the image became a great mountain and filled the whole earth."*[3] In symbol this stone is Jesus returning to earth, and the violent grinding and complete removal of the pieces graphically indicates the terrible devastation that will occur at the time. This is when the: *"God of heaven will set up a kingdom which shall never be destroyed; and the kingdom shall not be left to other people; it shall break in pieces and consume all these kingdoms, and it shall stand forever."*[4]

The New Testament confirms the violent end of human domination at the hand of the returned Jesus. Those who regard Jesus as the epitome of love and kindness see only one side of his character. The other side, shown at his return to a godless earth, is mentioned by the Apostle Paul: *"You who are*

---

1. Luke 12.32 **2.** Page 26 **3.** Daniel 2.35 **4.** Daniel 2.44

troubled rest with us when the Lord Jesus is revealed from heaven with His mighty angels, in flaming fire taking vengeance on those who do not know God, and on those who do not obey the gospel of our Lord Jesus Christ… And then the lawless one will be revealed, whom the Lord will consume with the breath of His mouth and destroy with the brightness of His coming."[1]

Similarly, the Book of Revelation chapter 19 describes the great and final Battle of Armageddon at which Jesus in symbol is seated on a white horse and: *"out of His mouth goes a sharp sword, that with it he should strike the nations. And he himself will rule them with a rod of iron. He himself treads the winepress of the fierceness and wrath of Almighty God."*[2]

As a result, all the wicked in the world will be removed, and Christ's reign of righteousness will spread throughout the earth, ruling over a purified and God-honouring population. This will be the Kingdom that Jesus bids us pray for.

Is your view of Christianity able to accept the full import of such passages as these?

---

1. 2 Thessalonians 1.7–8; 2.8 **2.** Revelation 19.15

Chapter 10
Final thoughts

Despite the fact that sometimes we are told for our comfort (and as a sop to other religions, or even to those who have no religion at all) "All roads lead to God", as far as the Bible is concerned Christianity is the only true religion. This was the message of the Apostles from the very first day it was preached. Speaking of Jesus, the Apostle Peter said: *"Nor is there salvation in any other, for there is **no other name** under heaven given among men by which we must be saved."*[1] Giving consideration to the claims of other religions may feel very charitable, but on the Apostles' (and therefore Christ's) authority they cannot bring the salvation from death that we all need.

But modern Christians cannot be complacent, for the teaching of organised Christianity today is a poor reflection of that original faith. As has been shown in the preceding pages, the original Christian message has been changed – and changed fundamentally. This is exactly as those early preachers predicted, and the New Testament contains many instances of these warnings. Paul wrote: *"For the time will come when they will not endure sound doctrine, but according to their own desires, because they have itching ears, they will heap up for themselves teachers; and they will turn their ears away from the truth, and be turned aside to fables."*[2]

Clearly there is a need to get back to the teaching and practices of the original Christians, and there are some Christian groups today whose aim is to do this – the writer being a member of one of them.

---

1. Acts 4.12 **2.** 2 Timothy 4.3; see also Acts 20.28–30; 2 Peter 2.1

So we ask you to really investigate the issues we have raised: to examine your beliefs with your Bible in hand. Your local church was not intended to be merely a social club – however pleasant that may be – but should be the means of bringing salvation and eternal life to individuals through the saving work of Jesus Christ. And that can only be done by being a real disciple – a follower – of him in all that he said and did.

Are you up to the challenge?

If you would like to receive further information on the subjects covered in this book please contact: The Dawn Book Supply, 5 Station Road, Carlton, Nottingham NG4 3AT or the address shown below:

Index of Bible references